KIND-NESS EVERY DAY

A JOURNAL

CHRONICLE BOOKS

SAN FRANCISCO

Text copyright © 2017 by Chronicle Books LLC.

All rights reserved. No part of this book may be reproduced in any
form without written permission from the publisher.

ISBN 978-1-4521-6305-5

Manufactured in China

MIX
Paper from
responsible sources
FSC™ C008047

Text by Carey Jones
Design by Allison Weiner

10 9 8 7 6 5 4 3 2 1

Chronicle Books LLC
680 Second Street
San Francisco, California 94107
www.chroniclebooks.com

PRACTICING
KINDNESS

What comes to mind when you hear the word *kindness*? You may think of other associated virtues: altruism, compassion, empathy, helpfulness, generosity, friendliness. Perhaps you remember a time when someone's words or actions made your day or week brighter. Being on the receiving end of kindness feels good, and as it turns out, there are many benefits to *practicing* kindness as well.

KINDNESS BRINGS US TOGETHER

The word *kindness* has the same root as the word *kin*. When we treat people with kindness, we are showing them the same warmth we'd offer to members of our own family.

By being kind to people, whether they are family, friends, or strangers, we are connecting with them, making them feel seen. Directing kindness, compassion, and love to yourself as well as others (even if you do it silently—a Buddhist practice known as loving-kindness meditation) has been shown to increase feelings of social connection and decrease negative biases. Practicing kindness can make a big world feel a bit smaller, even just for a few moments.

KINDNESS FIGHTS STRESS

Being kind to others can be a surprising form of stress relief. One study found that people who performed more kind acts than usual throughout their daily lives reported less stress and felt better equipped to deal with negative emotions. And the converse was found to be true: On days when study participants weren't able to be altruistic, their stress levels felt higher. Performing kind acts may spur the release of oxytocin, a calming hormone. Or it may be that when we do good deeds for others, we are less able to focus on our own problems.

KINDNESS MAKES US HAPPY

This one may seem obvious—being kind makes us feel good—but it's borne out by research as well. Dr. Sonja Lyubomirsky, professor of psychology at the University of California, Riverside, conducted a six-week study in which subjects were directed to do five random acts of kindness a week. At the end of the six weeks, Lyubomirsky found the subjects had become more than 40 percent happier. Other studies have shown, for both adults and children, that people who performed kind acts reported increased levels of happiness, heightened feelings of connectedness, and less depression.

KINDNESS IS CONTAGIOUS

The concept of "paying it forward" really does work. Studies show that acts of kindness can inspire recipients to act more generously, creating a continuous and spreading chain of more kindnesses. And it's not only the givers and receivers of kindness who benefit—even observers of kindness are impacted, and become kinder themselves. Being kind also makes you the sort of person that other people want to be around.

This journal is designed to help you cultivate more kindness in your life. In the pages that follow, you will find prompts for simple kindness exercises, along with inspiring and insightful quotes. Work through the journal from front to back, or flip through the pages and dip into exercises that particularly resonate with you. If you need more specific inspiration, see the list of Random Acts of Kindness on the following page, which offers easy yet meaningful ways to be kind.

Practicing kindness regularly—adopting a kindness habit, so to speak—will reap rewards for you (and others!) for years to come. Commit to kindness, and get ready to welcome lasting and positive change into your life.

RANDOM ACTS OF
KINDNESS

+ Leave an extra-large tip at a restaurant.

+ If someone is in need or grieving, help him or her.
Rather than saying, "Let me know if I can do anything," suggest specific ways you can contribute—
buying groceries, babysitting their children, running
errands.

+ Put spare change in a parking meter you see is about
to expire.

+ Offer to return someone's shopping cart on your way
into a grocery store.

+ Look a homeless person in the eye and smile when
you pass on the street.

+ Do something special on Mother's Day or Father's
Day for a friend who has lost a parent.

+ Donate to a charity.

+ When you enter a building, hold the door for people
behind you.

+ Help out senior citizens in your neighborhood. Run errands, carry groceries, give them a ride, help with yard work, cook them a hot meal.

+ Offer a drink to your mail carrier: something cold in summer, or warm in winter.

+ If a coworker does something you appreciate, tell his or her boss.

+ Learn the names of the people you are in regular contact with—your bus driver, the crossing guard at your child's school, your barista, your doorman—and greet them by name.

+ If you witness a child you know saying or doing something nice, let his or her parent know.

+ Let someone into your lane at rush hour.

+ Remember people's birthdays, and reach out to them with a card, call, text, or note on social media.

+ Leave spare change on a vending machine or at the laundromat.

+ On your way to the grocery store, drugstore, or warehouse club, call a friend and ask if you can pick up anything for her.

+ Hold the elevator (even when you'd rather not).

+ Give up your seat on a train or bus.

+ Be kind to customer service representatives, even if you are contacting them because you're frustrated with a product or service, and even if you don't like their answers.

+ Introduce yourself to neighbors or building mates you don't know.

+ Pay for the person behind you at the tollbooth (or behind you in line at the coffee shop, etc.).

+ Let someone else have his or her way.

+ Visit a nursing home, even if you don't know anyone there.

+ Leave positive comments on a blog post where there are many negative ones.

+ Give directions to lost tourists, even if you're in a hurry to get somewhere.

+ Offer your restaurant doggie bag (with untouched food) to someone in need of a meal.

+ Take part in an activity with your partner or friend that he or she really enjoys (even if you don't).

+ Offer to babysit (for free of course) so your friends with children can have a date night out.

+ Buy a drink from a child's lemonade stand.

+ Give someone the benefit of the doubt.

+ Respond to emails and voicemails quickly.

+ Lend your talents to someone else. Can you do someone's taxes? Help a friend build a website? Fix a leaky tap?

+ Be enthusiastic about your friends' successes.

+ If someone tells you a secret, keep it.

+ If your company allows it, donate sick days or vacation time to a coworker who needs them.

+ Don't be stingy.

+ Offer to help a friend do something he's been putting off.

Take a few minutes to write down what you hope to accomplish by keeping this journal. Do you want to increase your happiness? Fight stress? Create more community in your life? Make the world a better place? Whatever your reasons, keeping them in mind will help as you work through the journal.

WHAT YOU LEAVE BEHIND IS NOT WHAT IS ENGRAVED IN STONE MONUMENTS, BUT WHAT IS WOVEN INTO THE LIVES OF OTHERS. ~

PERICLES

Perform a random act of kindness today. (If you need an idea, refer to the Random Acts of Kindness list at the beginning of the journal.) How did it feel? What reaction did you get?

Offer a word of encouragement today. What was it?
How did it feel?

_____

_____

_____

_____

_____

_____

_____

_____

_____

_____

_____

_____

_____

_____

CONSTANT
KINDNESS
CAN ACCOMPLISH MUCH.
AS THE SUN MAKES ICE
MELT, KINDNESS CAUSES
MISUNDER-
STANDING,
MISTRUST,
AND HOSTILITY TO
EVAPORATE.

ALBERT SCHWEITZER

Are there any instances of misunderstanding, mistrust, or hostility in your life that you could heal with kindness?

_____

_____

_____

_____

_____

_____

_____

_____

_____

_____

_____

_____

_____

_____

Make a list of some memorable kind things people have
done for you. How did these acts change you?

Make a list of some memorable kind things *you* have done for others. How did these acts change you?

Make a list of some memorable kind thoughts that
people have expressed to you. How did these words
change you?

_____

_____

_____

_____

_____

_____

_____

_____

_____

_____

_____

_____

_____

_____

WHEREVER THERE IS A
HUMAN BEING,
THERE IS AN
OPPORTUNITY
FOR A
KINDNESS.

LUCIUS ANNAEUS SENECA

Make a list of some memorable kind words *you* have
said to others. How did saying these words change you?

Help someone today. What did you do? How did it feel?

Think of someone you've taken for granted. Make it a point today to let them know how you feel.

Give someone a compliment today. What was it? How did it feel?

BY SWALLOWING
EVIL WORDS
UNSAID, NO ONE
HAS EVER HARMED
HIS STOMACH.

WINSTON CHURCHILL

See if you can go a whole day without saying something
negative. Write about the experience here.

IF YOUR
COMPASSION
DOES NOT INCLUDE
YOURSELF, IT IS
INCOMPLETE.

BUDDHA

Self-kindness is just as important as being kind to others. Can you think of ways you would like to be more kind to yourself?

Surprise a friend today with a little gift "just because." It doesn't have to be expensive, just something to show you care. Write about it here.

Help someone today. What did you do? How did it feel?

Make someone feel important today. Praise a colleague;
give a friend your undivided attention; let someone
solve a problem for you.

Don't forget common courtesy: This week, make it a point to include *please* and *thank you* in your interactions with friends and strangers alike.

THAT **BEST**
PORTION OF A
GOOD MAN'S
LIFE, HIS LITTLE,
NAMELESS,
UNREMEMBERED
ACTS OF
KINDNESS
AND **LOVE.** ~

WILLIAM WORDSWORTH

Offering your trust can be a form of kindness. This
week, trust someone—with a secret, with something
that belongs to you, or with a responsibility. Write
about it here.

Oftentimes we are courteous to strangers but can forget to be kind to our own family. Think about this the next time you are frustrated or angry with your spouse or parent or child.

Offer a word of encouragement today. What was it?
How did it feel?

A GOOD CHARACTER IS THE BEST
TOMBSTONE. THOSE WHO LOVED
YOU AND WERE HELPED BY YOU
WILL REMEMBER YOU WHEN
FORGET-ME-NOTS HAVE WITHERED.

CARVE YOUR NAME ON HEARTS, NOT ON MARBLE.

CHARLES H. SPURGEON

The next time you hear a friend complain about a problem he or she is having, see if you can go beyond sympathy. Can you help fix the problem?

Help someone today. What did you do? How did it feel?

This week, do a favor for someone you love, even if it is inconvenient for you.

THREE THINGS IN HUMAN LIFE ARE IMPORTANT. THE FIRST IS TO BE KIND. THE SECOND IS TO BE KIND. AND THE THIRD IS TO BE KIND.

HENRY JAMES

Perform a random act of kindness today. How did it feel? What reaction did you get?

Try this kindness exercise the next time you are with a group of people, whether they are family members, friends, or colleagues: Give each person a sheet of paper and ask them to write down something they admire, like, or value about each other person in the group. Compile all the compliments and pass them out to each person. (You may decide as a group if you want to share the compliments out loud.)

DATE / /

HUMAN KINDNESS HAS
NEVER WEAKENED THE
STAMINA OR SOFTENED THE
FIBER OF A FREE PEOPLE.
A NATION
DOES NOT
HAVE TO BE
CRUEL TO
BE TOUGH.

FRANKLIN D. ROOSEVELT

The next time you have to stand up to someone or have a difficult conversation, think about the interplay of kindness and toughness. Can you be both at the same time?

_____

_____

_____

_____

_____

_____

_____

_____

_____

_____

_____

_____

_____

IN **THIS WORLD,** YOU MUST BE A BIT **TOO KIND** IN ORDER TO BE **KIND ENOUGH.**

PIERRE CARLET DE CHAMBLAIN DE MARIVAUX

Give someone a compliment today. What was it? How did it feel?

_____

_____

_____

_____

_____

_____

_____

_____

_____

_____

_____

_____

_____

IT IS ONE OF THE MOST
BEAUTIFUL
COMPENSATIONS OF
LIFE THAT NO MAN
CAN SINCERELY
TRY TO HELP
ANOTHER WITH-
OUT HELPING HIMSELF.

RALPH WALDO EMERSON

Research shows that smiling can make you feel happier—
and can make those around you feel good as well. The
next time you are in a bad mood, try smiling at people
around you, even if it feels forced. Does it change your
spirits?

Offer a word of encouragement today. What was it?
How did it feel?

People often have an easier time accepting criticism when it is offered along with positive comments. Think about this the next time you have to give difficult feedback to someone. Can you think of positive (yet truthful and sincere) ways to couch the information you need to convey?

HOW LOVELY THAT EVERYONE, GREAT AND SMALL, CAN MAKE THEIR CONTRIBUTION TOWARD INTRODUCING JUSTICE STRAIGHTAWAY. AND YOU CAN ALWAYS, ALWAYS GIVE SOMETHING, EVEN IF IT IS ONLY KINDNESS!

ANNE FRANK

Perform a random act of kindness today. How did it feel? What reaction did you get?

Make a list of three people you know whose kindness
you admire. What can you do to emulate them?

Help someone today. What did you do? How did it feel?

KIND DEEDS OFTEN COME BACK TO THE GIVERS IN FAIRER SHAPES THAN THEY GO.

LOUISA MAY ALCOTT

Forgiving someone is a type of kindness. Can you think
of someone you need to forgive?

Can you make kindness contagious? When someone is kind to you this week, pay it forward by doing something kind for another person.

Offer a word of encouragement today. What was it?
How did it feel?

SO MANY GODS,
SO MANY CREEDS,
SO MANY PATHS
THAT WIND AND WIND,
WHILE JUST THE
ART OF BEING KIND
IS ALL THE SAD
WORLD NEEDS.

ELLA WHEELER WILCOX

Try having a respectful conversation with someone of a different political or religious viewpoint. Can you find common ground despite your differences?

This week, give something away that costs you nothing—
a kind intention, a smile, a word of advice. How does
it feel?

'TIS ONLY NOBLE
TO BE GOOD.
KIND HEARTS
ARE MORE THAN
CORONETS.

ALFRED, LORD TENNYSON

This week, give something away that does cost you
something. How does it feel?

A KIND WORD IS LIKE A SPRING DAY.

RUSSIAN PROVERB

Offer a word of encouragement today. What was it?
How did it feel?

Help someone today. What did you do? How did it feel?

ONE GOOD TURN DESERVES ANOTHER.

ENGLISH PROVERB

This week, let someone help you. How does it feel?

I FEEL THE
CAPACITY
TO CARE IS
THE THING WHICH
GIVES LIFE ITS
DEEPEST
SIGNIFICANCE.

PABLO CASALS

This week, take time to listen—without interrupting—to someone going through a tough time.

Give someone a compliment today. What was it? How
did it feel?

BE KIND,
FOR EVERYONE
YOU MEET IS
FIGHTING
A HARD BATTLE.

IAN MACLAREN

The next time you have an unpleasant interaction with someone, remind yourself that the other person may be "fighting a hard battle." Can you respond with kindness instead of harsh words?

Smile and say hello to five strangers today.

Offer a word of encouragement today. What was it?
How did it feel?

Help someone today. What did you do? How did it feel?

YOU CAN **ACCOMPLISH** BY **KINDNESS** WHAT YOU CANNOT BY **FORCE.**

PUBLILIUS SYRUS

Can you think of an instance in which you could
approach with kindness rather than with force?

Give someone a compliment today. What was it? How did it feel?

KINDNESS
IS IN OUR POWER, EVEN WHEN
FONDNESS
IS NOT.

SAMUEL JOHNSON

When someone irritates you, make a list of his or her
good qualities, or think of instances when he or she
was helpful to you. Does this activity change your
thinking or mood?

WHAT **WISDOM** CAN YOU FIND THAT IS **GREATER** THAN **KINDNESS?**

JEAN-JACQUES ROUSSEAU

Perform a random act of kindness today. How did it feel? What reaction did you get?

This week, do a kind act for someone you know, and
then do the same kind act for a stranger. How did it feel
to do both?

Offer a word of encouragement today. What was it?
How did it feel?

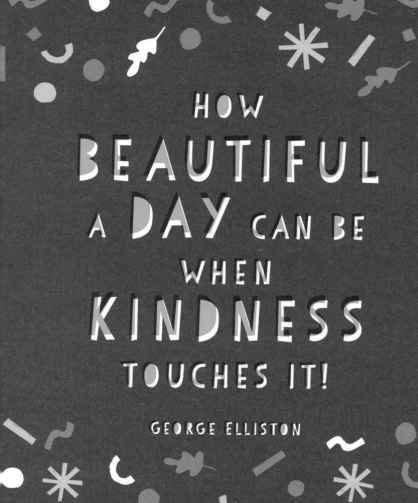

HOW
BEAUTIFUL
A DAY CAN BE
WHEN
KINDNESS
TOUCHES IT!

GEORGE ELLISTON

DATE / /

How can you make someone's day better today?

HOW **FAR** THAT
LITTLE **CANDLE**
THROWS HIS
BEAMS!
SO SHINES A
GOOD DEED IN A
NAUGHTY
WORLD.

WILLIAM SHAKESPEARE

Perform a random act of kindness today. How did it feel? What reaction did you get?

KIND WORDS WILL UNLOCK AN IRON DOOR.

KURDISH PROVERB

Cooperating is a way of being kind. The next time you have to work with someone on a project or solve a problem together, can you use kindness as your guiding principle?

Give someone a compliment today. What was it? How did it feel?

ANY **KINDNESS**
I CAN SHOW TO
ANY **FELLOW**
CREATURE,
LET ME DO IT NOW.
LET ME NOT DEFER
OR NEGLECT IT, FOR
I SHALL NOT PASS
THIS WAY **AGAIN.**

STEPHEN GRELLET

Is there something kind you have been meaning to do
for or say to someone? Can you do it today?

Help someone today. What did you do? How did it feel?

NO ACT OF KINDNESS, NO MATTER HOW SMALL, IS EVER WASTED.

AESOP

The next time you see someone you don't like, go out of your way to be kind. Offer a compliment or inquire sincerely about the person's family. Do you feel differently after the interaction when you are kind? Did the person respond to you differently?

Perform a random act of kindness today. How did it feel? What reaction did you get?

THE **SECRET** OF **CHANGE** IS TO FOCUS ALL YOUR ENERGY NOT ON **FIGHTING** THE OLD BUT ON BUILDING THE **NEW.**

DAN MILLMAN

Let go of a lingering grudge or resentment—it is a way to be kind to yourself as well as others. Does it help you move forward?

_____

_____

_____

_____

_____

_____

_____

_____

_____

_____

_____

_____

_____

Offer a word of encouragement today. What was it?
How did it feel?

BE NICE
TO PEOPLE
ON YOUR WAY
UP
BECAUSE YOU'LL
MEET THEM ON
YOUR WAY
DOWN.

WILSON MIZNER

Today, say thank you to people who do jobs that are often overlooked: janitors, security guards, restaurant bussers, grocery cashiers.

Give someone a compliment today. What was it? How did it feel?

_____

_____

_____

_____

_____

_____

_____

_____

_____

_____

_____

_____

_____

_____

Help someone today. What did you do? How did it feel?

GENEROSITY DOES **NOT** MAKE A MAN **POORER.**

YIDDISH PROVERB

Perform a random act of kindness today. How did it feel? What reaction did you get?

NO MAN is USELESS WHILE HE HAS A FRIEND.

ROBERT LOUIS STEVENSON

Offer to take a new coworker or classmate out for coffee
this week.

Offer a word of encouragement today. What was it?
How did it feel?

_____

_____

_____

_____

_____

_____

_____

_____

_____

_____

_____

_____

_____

_____

THERE ARE TWO WAYS OF SPREAD-ING LIGHT; TO BE THE CANDLE OR THE MIRROR THAT REFLECTS IT.

EDITH WHARTON

This week, when you are feeling frustrated or angry or sad, make it a point to be kind to another person. Does it change your outlook on life?

- -

- -

- -

- -

- -

- -

- -

- -

- -

- -

- -

Help someone today. What did you do? How did it feel?

Volunteer your time to do charity work this month.

DATE / /

Give someone a compliment today. What was it? How did it feel? How did he or she react?

_____

_____

_____

_____

_____

_____

_____

_____

_____

_____

_____

_____

_____

_____

SHALL WE MAKE A NEW RULE OF LIFE FROM TONIGHT: ALWAYS TO TRY TO BE A LITTLE KINDER THAN IS NECESSARY?

J. M. BARRIE

The next time you're with people who are gossiping,
don't join in. Redirect the conversation. What happens?

Perform a random act of kindness today. How did it feel? What reaction did you get?

SO LONG

AS YOU CAN

SWEETEN

ANOTHER'S PAIN,

LIFE IS

NOT IN VAIN.

HELEN KELLER

Make a point this week to help someone who is in pain.

Kindness need not be restricted to people. This week, think of a way to direct kindness toward the planet (pick up trash around your neighborhood, recycle) or other beings (volunteer at an animal shelter, play with a friend's dog).

DEEDS OF
KINDNESS
ARE EQUAL IN WEIGHT
TO ALL THE
COMMANDMENTS.

THE TALMUD

How can you make someone happy today?

Offer a word of encouragement today. What was it?
How did it feel?

COMPASSION IS THE CHIEF LAW OF HUMAN EXISTENCE.

FYODOR DOSTOYEVSKY

People often respond to the greeting *How are you?* with the pat response *I'm fine*, even if they aren't. This week, when you greet people, look for any emotion behind their words that you could respond to with compassion.

_____

_____

_____

_____

_____

_____

_____

_____

_____

_____

_____

IT SPEAKS WELL FOR THE **NATIVE KINDNESS** OF OUR HEARTS, THAT NOTHING GIVES US GREATER PLEASURE THAN TO FEEL THAT WE ARE CONFERRING **IT**.

CHRISTIAN NESTELL BOVEE

Perform a random act of kindness today. How did it feel? What reaction did you get?

Give someone a compliment today. What was it? How did it feel?

LIFE IS MADE UP, NOT OF GREAT SACRIFICES OR DUTIES, BUT OF LITTLE THINGS, IN WHICH SMILES AND KINDNESS, AND SMALL OBLIGATIONS GIVEN HABITUALLY, ARE WHAT PRESERVE THE HEART AND SECURE COMFORT.

HUMPHRY DAVY

Let someone go ahead of you in line this week.

Help someone today. What did you do? How did it feel?

WE CANNOT TELL THE PRECISE
MOMENT WHEN FRIENDSHIP IS
FORMED. AS IN FILLING A VESSEL
DROP BY DROP,
THERE IS AT LAST A DROP WHICH
MAKES IT RUN OVER;
SO IN A SERIES OF KINDNESSES
THERE IS AT LAST ONE
WHICH MAKES THE
HEART RUN OVER.

JAMES BOSWELL

Reach out to a friend today for no reason other than just to let her know you were thinking of her.

Give someone a compliment today. What was it? How did it feel?

A BIT OF FRAGRANCE CLINGS TO THE HAND THAT GIVES FLOWERS.

CHINESE PROVERB

Take time to teach someone something today.

This week, tell someone about something you learned
from him or her.

_____

_____

_____

_____

_____

_____

_____

_____

_____

_____

_____

_____

_____

REAL GENEROSITY IS DOING SOMETHING NICE FOR SOMEONE WHO WILL NEVER FIND OUT.

FRANK A. CLARK

This week, perform a secret act of kindness for someone.

Offer a word of encouragement today. What was it?
How did it feel?

Perform a random act of kindness today. How did it feel? What reaction did you get?

Give someone a compliment today. What was it? How
did it feel?

NEVER LOSE
A CHANCE OF
SAYING A KIND
WORD.

WILLIAM MAKEPEACE THACKERAY

Laughter releases dopamine and activates the brain's pleasure center. Can you lift someone's mood today by making him or her laugh? Write about it here.

Help someone today. What did you do? How did it feel?

Perform a random act of kindness today. How did it feel? What reaction did you get?

Give someone a compliment today. What was it? How did it feel?

_____

_____

_____

_____

_____

_____

_____

_____

_____

_____

_____

_____

_____

_____

Help someone today. What did you do? How did it feel?

THE SMALLEST ACT OF KINDNESS IS WORTH MORE THAN THE GREAT-EST INTENTION.

KAHLIL GIBRAN

While it feels good to accomplish something, it can be just as rewarding to hear that someone else noticed. This week, give someone credit for an accomplishment.

Perform a random act of kindness today. How did it feel? What reaction did you get?

Offer a word of encouragement today. What was it?
How did it feel?

_____

_____

_____

_____

_____

_____

_____

_____

_____

_____

_____

_____

_____

_____

You can show kindness by being reliable for the people in your life. This week, make an extra effort to be on time, do what you say you will, and be dependable in all areas of your life.

A SINGLE ACT

OF KINDNESS THROWS OUT
ROOTS IN ALL DIRECTIONS, AND
THE **ROOTS** SPRING
UP AND **MAKE NEW
TREES.** THE GREATEST
WORK THAT KINDNESS DOES
TO OTHERS IS THAT IT MAKES
THEM KIND THEMSELVES.

FREDERICK WILLIAM FABER

Offer a word of encouragement today. What was it?
How did it feel?

Give someone a compliment today. What was it? How did it feel?

Write a note to someone today for no other reason than
to thank him or her for being in your life.

DATE / /

Perform a random act of kindness today. How did it feel? What reaction did you get?